Created with love and care by Crumps Cottage Publishing
www.crumpscottage.com

Copyright © 2024 Crumps Cottage Publishing

All rights reserved. No part of this publication may be reproduced, distributed or transmitted in any form or by any means without prior written permission from the copyright holder, except for the use of brief quotations in critical reviews and certain non-commercial uses permitted by copyright law.

Although we make every effort to ensure that the information contained within this publication is correct at time of print we do not assume and hereby disclaim any liability to any party for any loss, damage or disruption caused by errors and omissions, whether such errors or omissions result from negligence, accident, or any other cause.

The content of this publication is presented solely for informational purposes.

To request permissions or provide feedback on the publication please contact:
hello@crumpscottage.com

Easter Egg Hunt

7

Use the compass and key to discover where the mischievous Easter Bunny has hidden the eggs on the farm. When you get to a square with a picture, use the directions on the key and follow the map to uncover the location of the tasty treats!

The Key:

 Go North at trees

 Go East at chickens

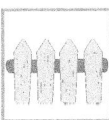 Go South at fences

 Go West at cows

Where has the Easter Bunny hidden the eggs?

A.  In the watering can

B.  Behind the barn

C.  Under the tractor

Egg-cellent Pairs

Connect the matching eggs by drawing a line between the boxes, but here's the twist: only hop straight up, down, or side-to-side. No sneaky diagonals or crossing through other egg paths allowed!

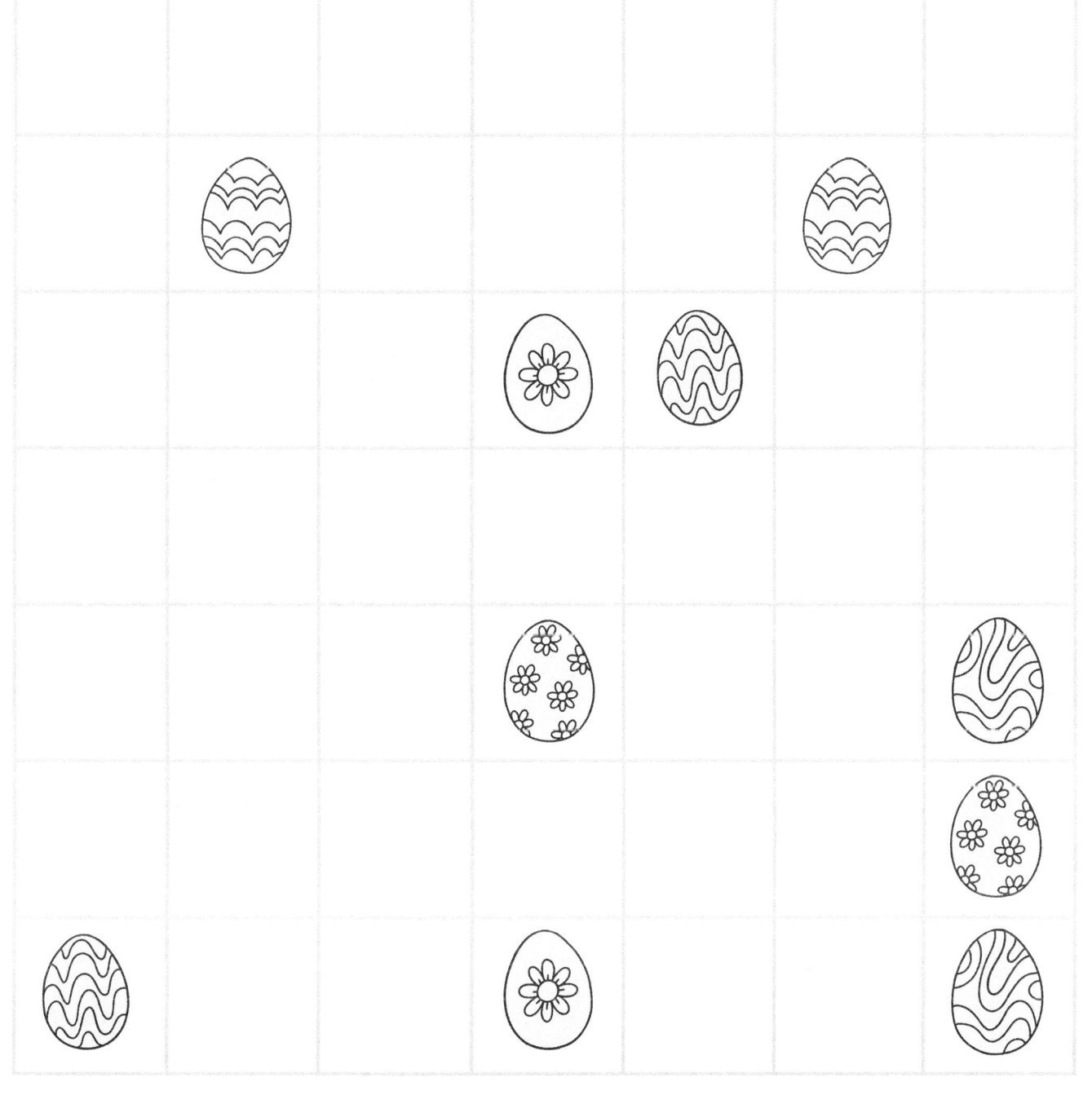

Secret Messages

The Easter bunny has left a secret message hidden across two boxes. Imagine the two boxes below together so that the blank squares in Box A are filled with the matching pieces from Box B. Can you crack the Easter Bunny's code and unveil the hidden message?

Box A

Box B

The secret message says:

One of these Easter trees is different. Circle the odd tree out.

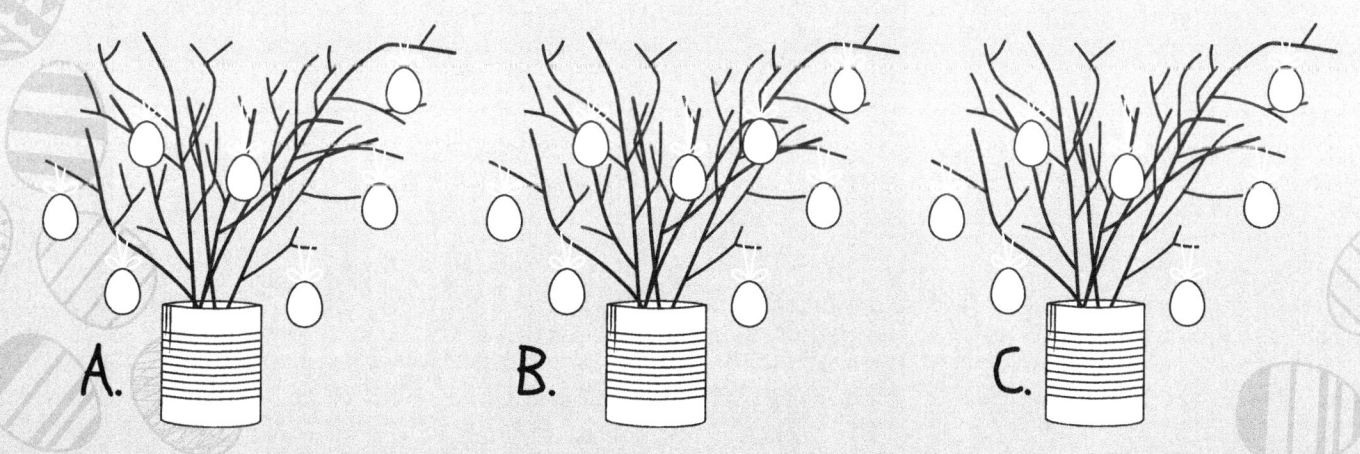

A.   B.   C.

Egg-citing Maze

Find your way through this egg-citing Easter Egg maze.

CRACKING JOKES
Q: What do you call an Easter Egg from outer space?
A: An egg-straterrestrial!

Spot The Difference

Circle the five differences in the above and below pictures of a basket of tasty Easter eggs.

Easter Riddle

Use the picto alphabet to figure out the answer to this Easter riddle; "How many Easter Eggs can you put in an empty basket?"

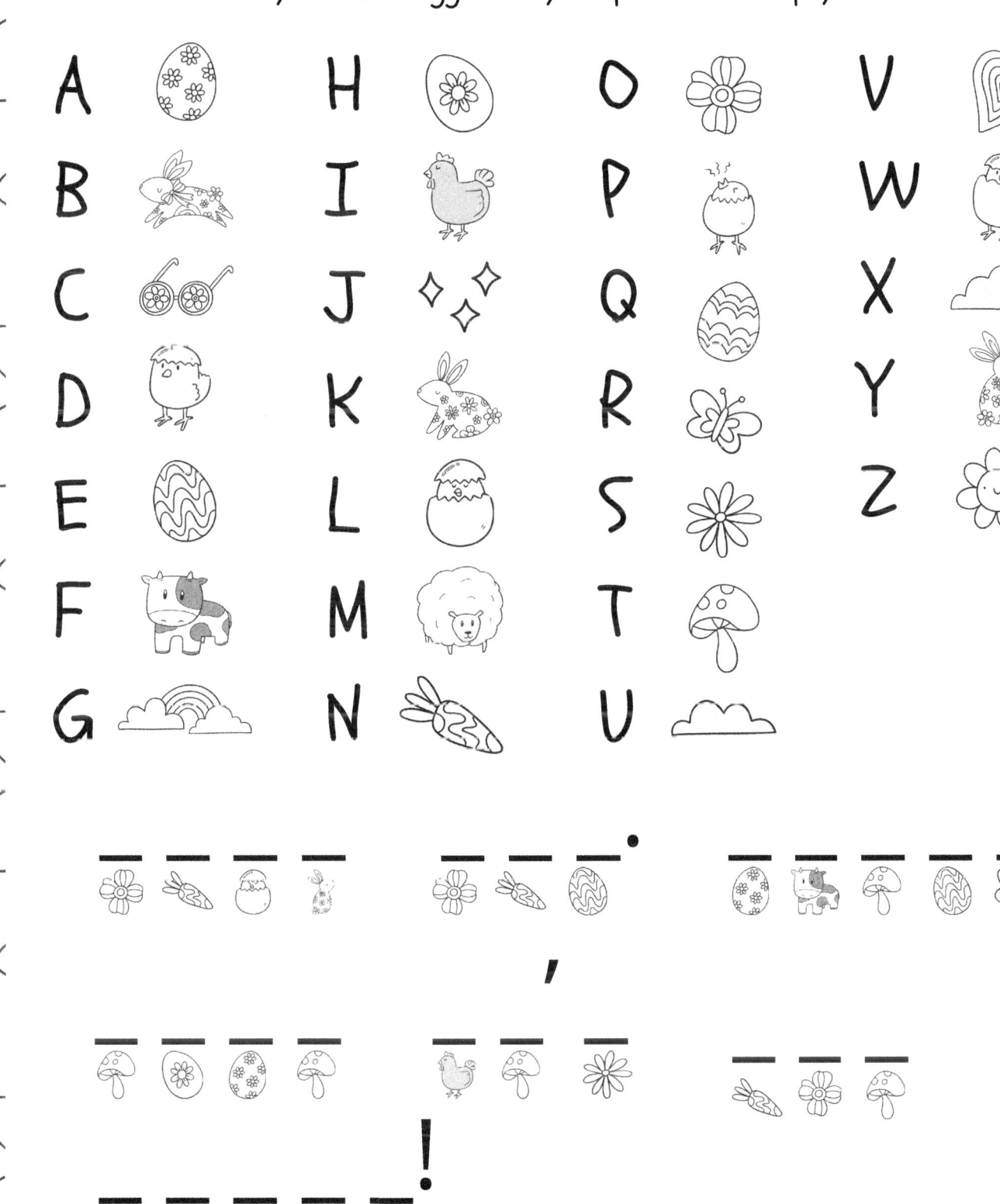

Design Your Egg

Let your creativity bloom by adding your own egg-cellent pattern to the Easter Egg below. Add some colour to make your picture egg-stra special!

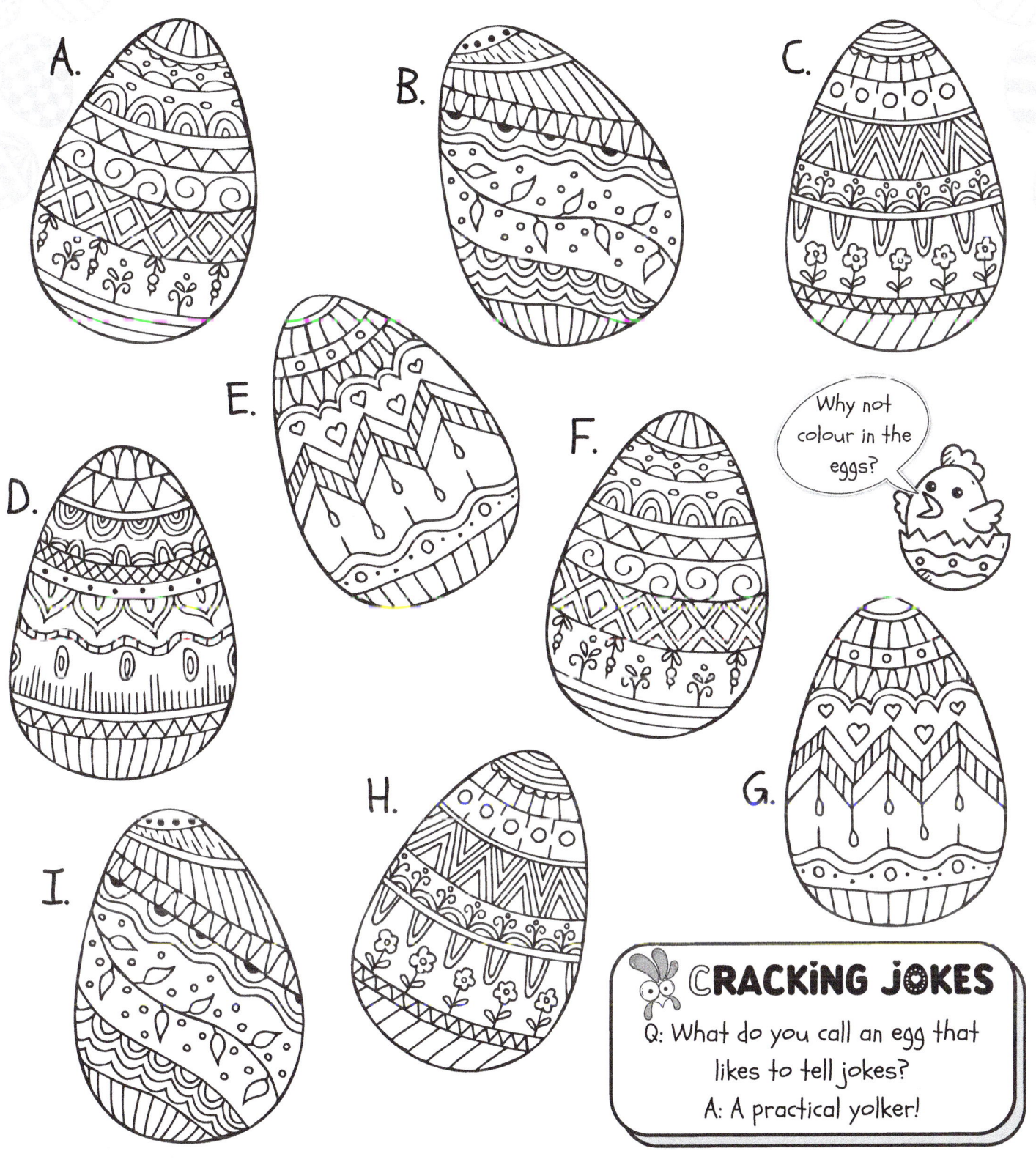

Animals On The Loose

23

The cheeky farm animals have all managed to get into the same field! Can you draw three straight lines to fence off the field into four sections? You must make sure that every section has one of each animal.

A naughty little bunny has covered up all the vowels (the letters A, E, I, O and U) from these two Easter activities. Work out what vowels are missing to complete the words.

1. ■■ST■R   ■GG   H■NT
   _____   _____   _____

2. ■GG   ■ND   SP■■N   R■C■
   _____   _____   _____   _____

Egg & Spoon Race

It's the egg and spoon race showdown, but there's a scramble to find the right route to the finish line! Which eager egg-racer will successfully find their way to victory?

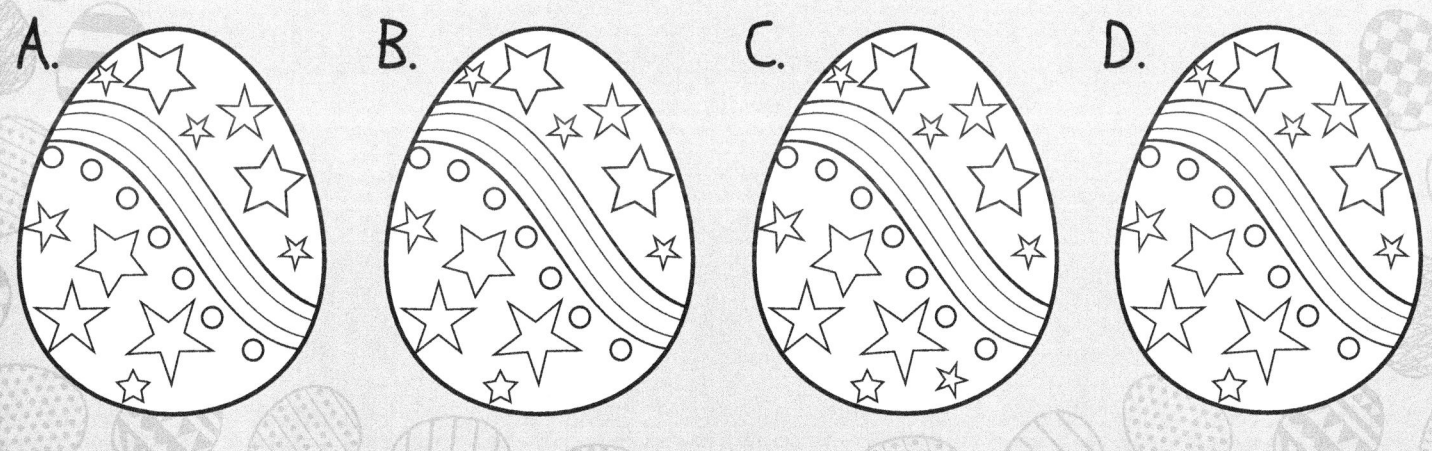

One of these Easter Eggs is different. Circle the odd egg out.

A.   B.   C.   D.

Sheep Squares Scramble

Take turns drawing straight lines between two sheep buddies that are side by side (not diagonal). When you complete all four sides of a square, hop in and mark it with your initials. Keep going and have another go. At the end, count up your squares – the player with the most squares takes home the prize for the woolliest win!

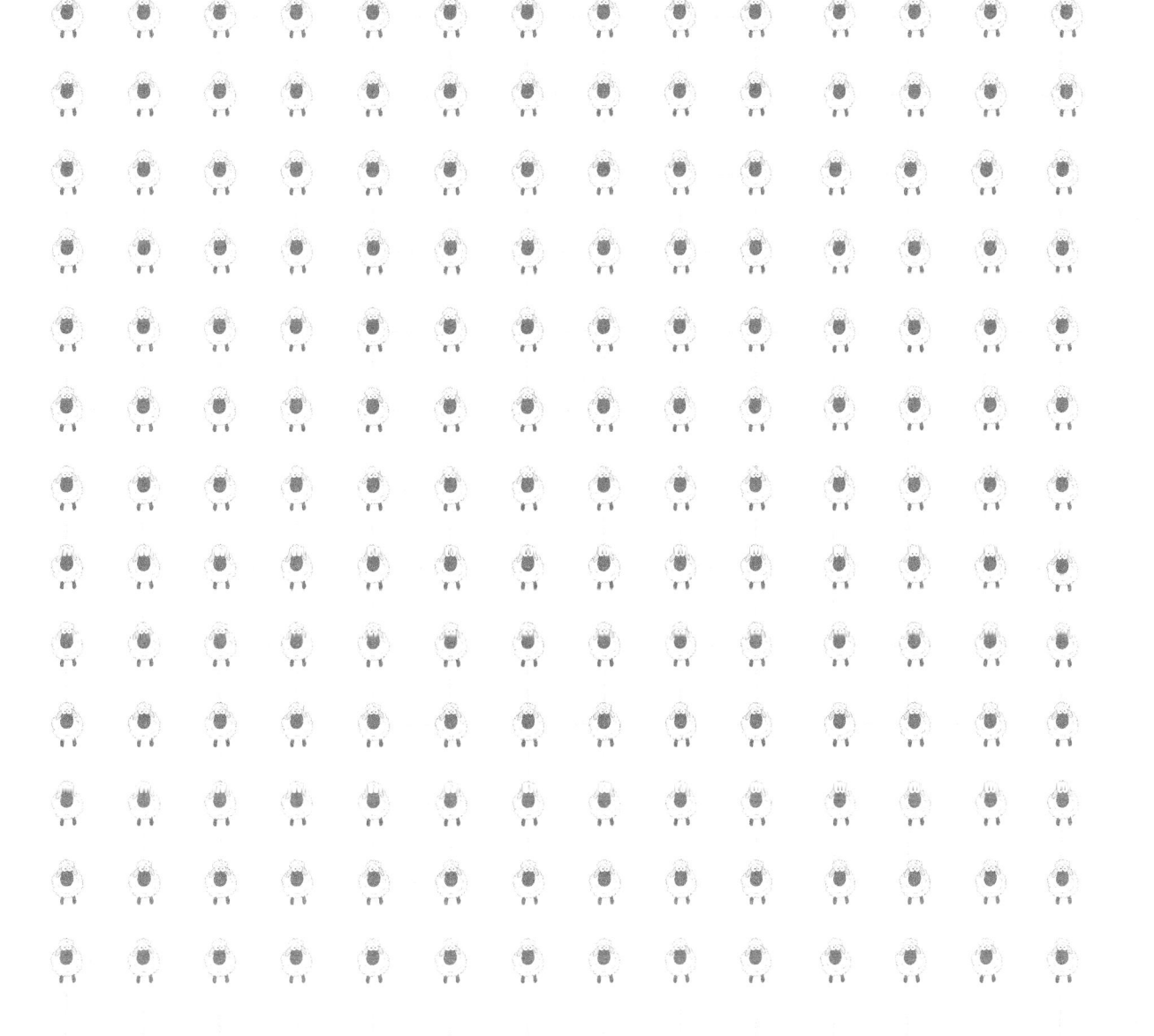

CRACKING JOKES
Q: Where do sheep watch videos online?
A: EweTube!

Connect The Dots

Connect the dots to discover which animal is hiding amongst the carrots and then colour it in to bring this Easter picture to life.

Easter Spy

33

Colour in an egg every time you spot one of the items below this Easter.

CRACKING JOKES
Q: What day are eggs scared of?
A: Fry-days!

Write the first letter of each object in the box below the picture to discover the answer to this math's riddle;

"Lily has 4 Easter eggs. Henry has 3 more Easter eggs than Lily. Josh has 2 less Easter eggs than Lily. Seb has 6 more Easter eggs than Josh. How many Easter eggs do they all have in total?"

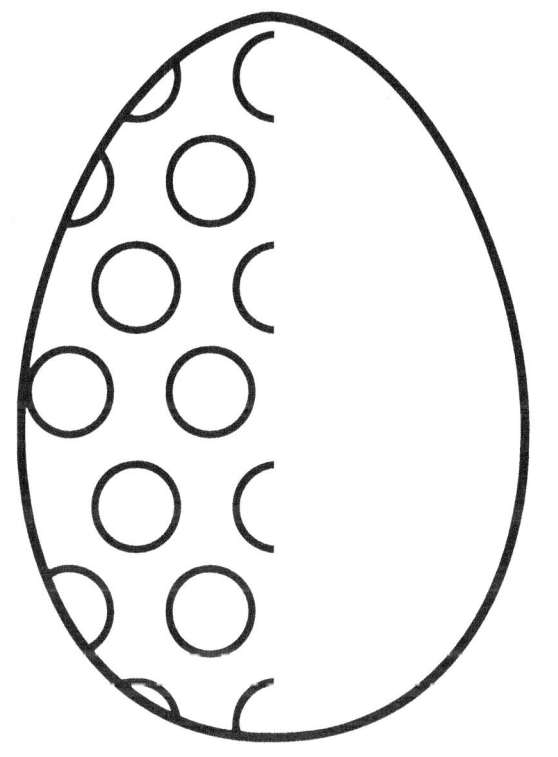
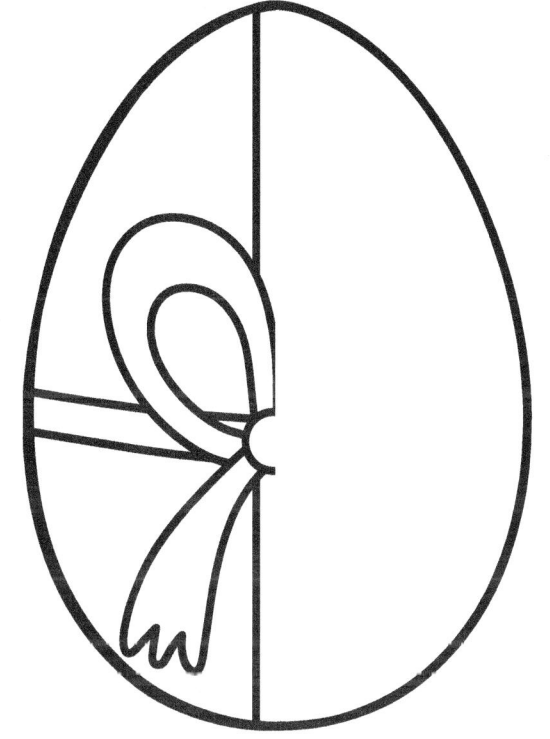

Easter Egg Symmetry

Let's hatch a plan for some egg-cellent symmetry fun! Can you draw and colour the eggs so that each side looks exactly the same?

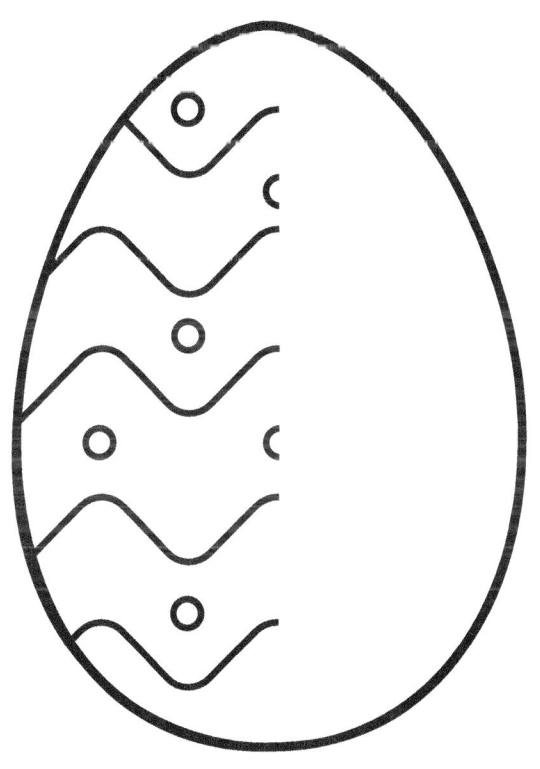
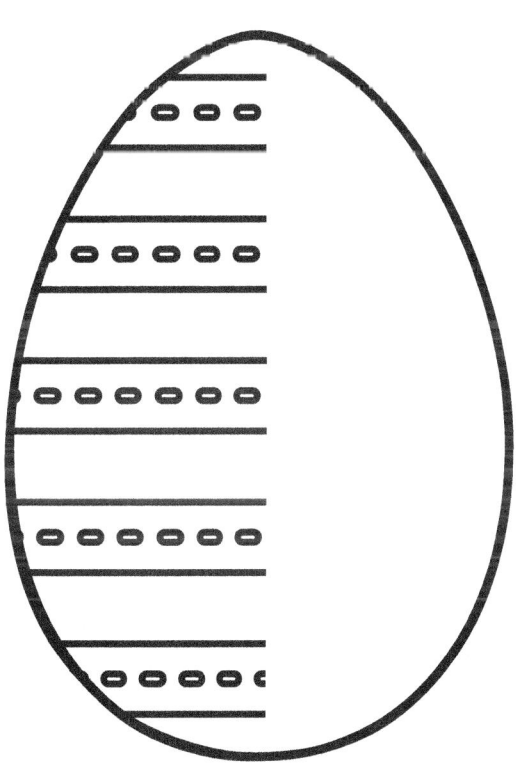

Chicken vs Egg

Compete head to head to finally settle the question; 'Who came first? The Chicken or the Egg?' Colour in and cut out the chicken and egg counters and take it in turns to place them on the squares. The winner is the first to make a line of three. So who will come first – the chicken or the egg?

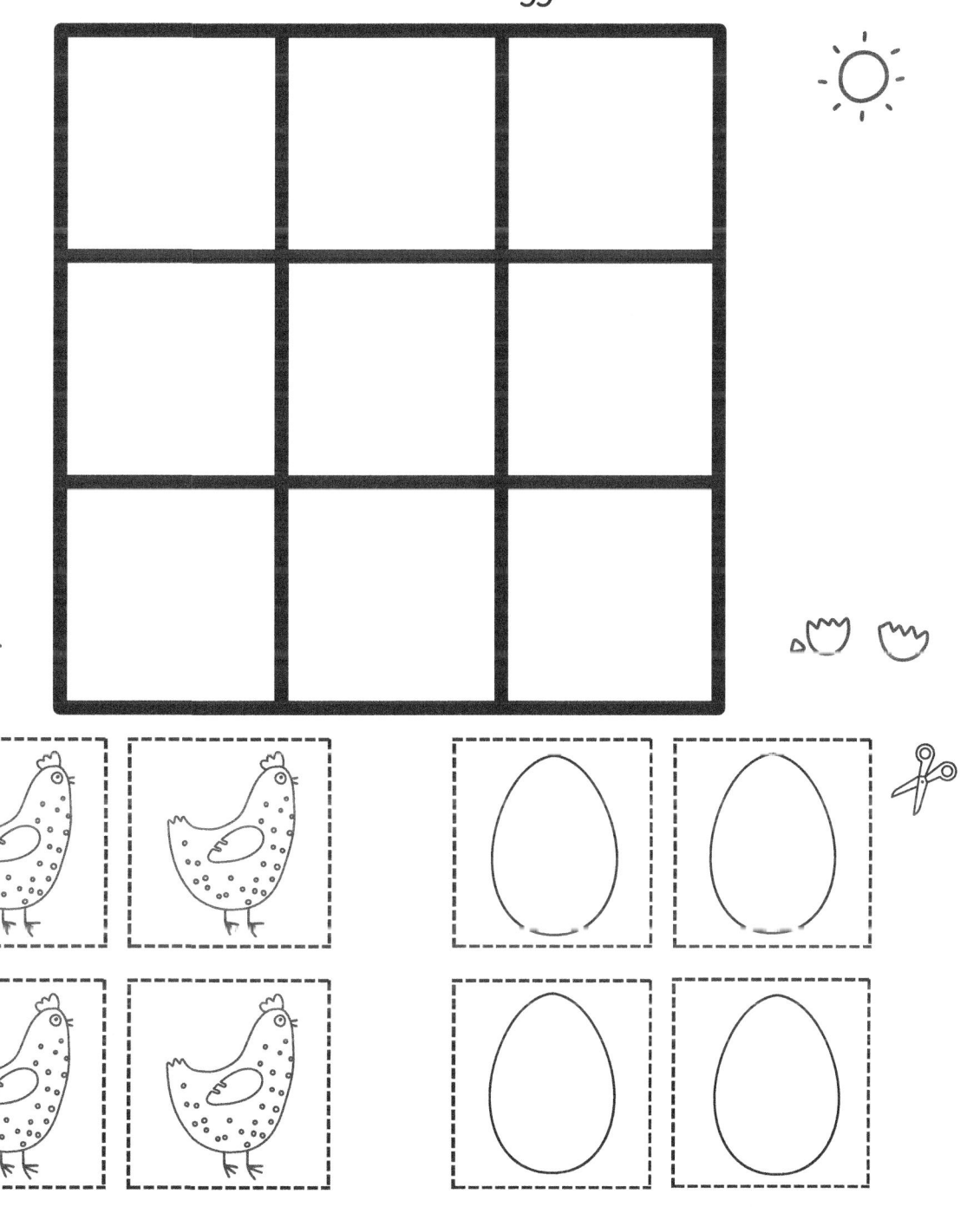

	A	B	C	D
1				
2				
3				
4				
5				

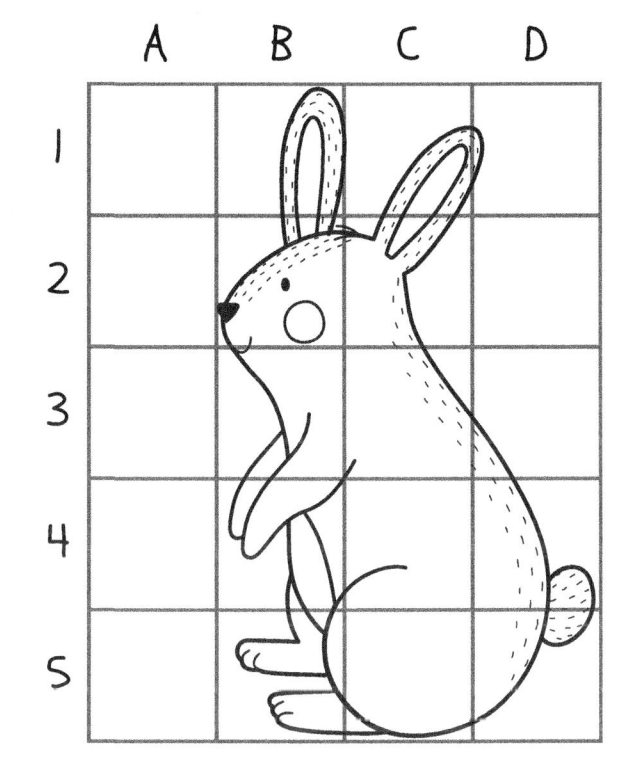

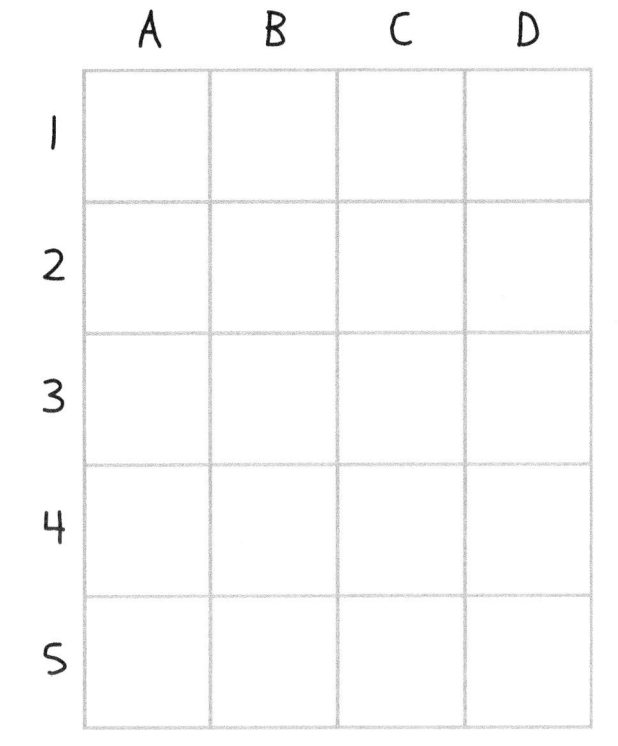

	A	B	C	D
1				
2				
3				
4				
5				

Easter Doodles

Use the grids to help you copy the drawing of a rabbit. Then follow the steps below to draw your own Easter doodle of a chicken.

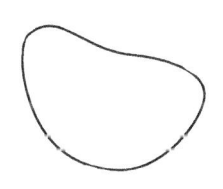

1. Draw the body

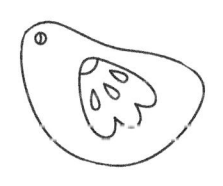

2. Add the wing and the eye

3. Add the legs

4. Add the beak, comb and tail

Hide Your Own Eggs

Colour in the garden and the three eggs at the bottom. Then cut out the eggs and stick them in the garden. Let's make this Easter scene bloom!

Easter Word Hunt

43

Can you hunt out all of these Easter words hiding in the word search?

F	V	H	U	H	Y	Z	Z	T	T	H	L
E	R	G	D	U	K	M	T	F	L	Q	M
V	L	B	E	N	S	P	R	I	N	G	Q
A	C	U	C	T	W	L	P	H	W	H	N
B	H	N	O	P	D	E	N	S	F	H	F
G	O	N	R	B	V	G	T	P	H	O	P
B	C	Y	A	A	M	G	I	M	H	B	X
J	O	K	T	S	U	S	J	T	C	S	U
T	L	M	E	K	V	A	W	Y	F	I	Y
M	A	E	Q	E	C	R	M	V	P	T	R
D	T	H	Y	T	B	O	N	N	E	T	T
O	E	C	M	K	M	J	T	U	S	G	U

BASKET   BONNET   BUNNY
CHOCOLATE   DECORATE   EGGS
HOP   HUNT   SPRING

Scrambled Eggs

45

Colour in these Easter pictures, then put your puzzle-solving skills to the test as you unscramble the hidden words.

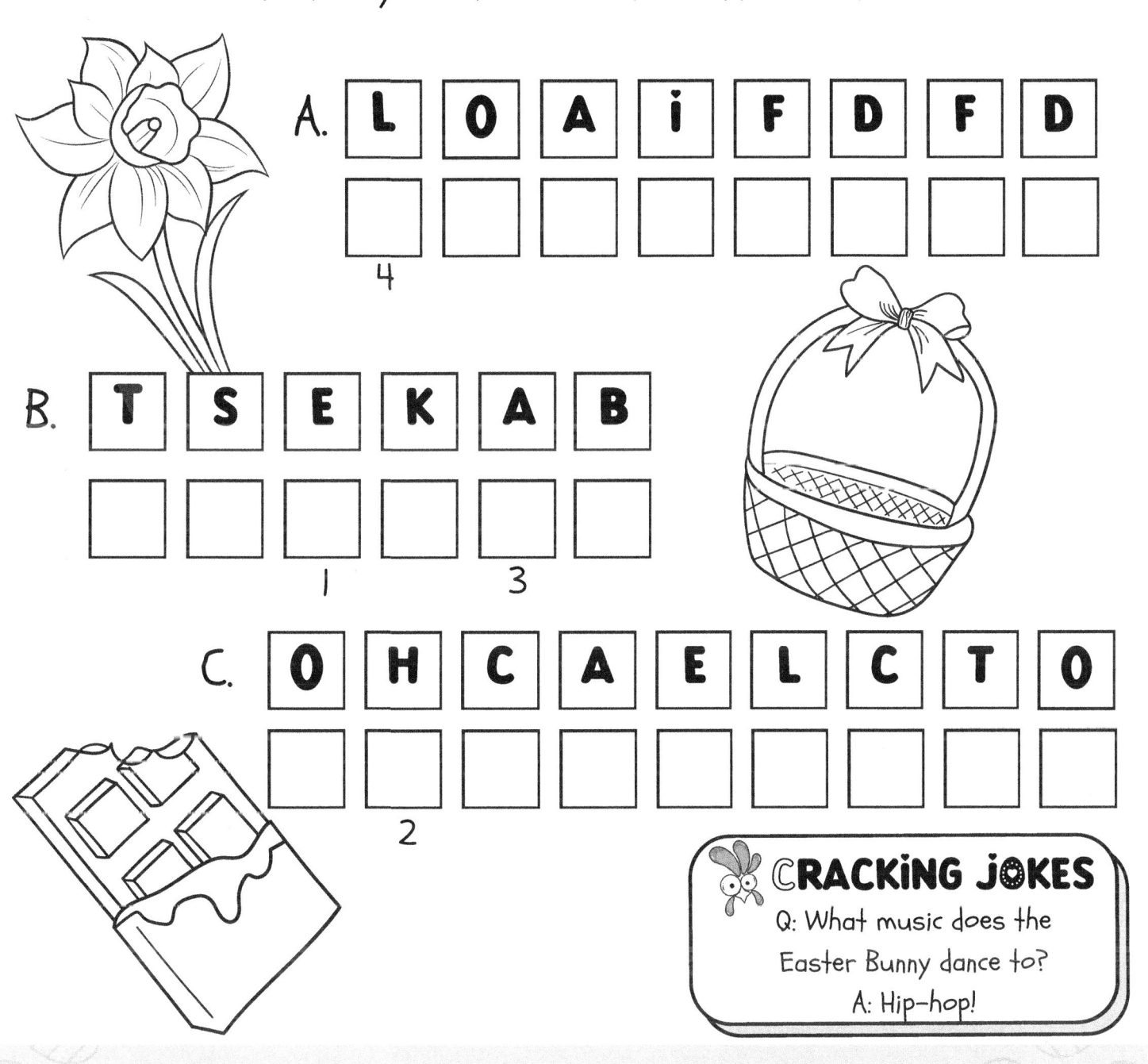

A. L O A I F D F D

4

B. T S E K A B

1   3

C. O H C A E L C T O

2

CRACKING JOKES
Q: What music does the Easter Bunny dance to?
A: Hip-hop!

Use the numbers below the unscrambled letters above to discover the Easter Egg's secret hiding place.

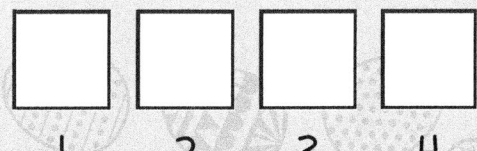

1 2 3 4

Bunny Maze

Hop your way through this Easter Bunny maze.

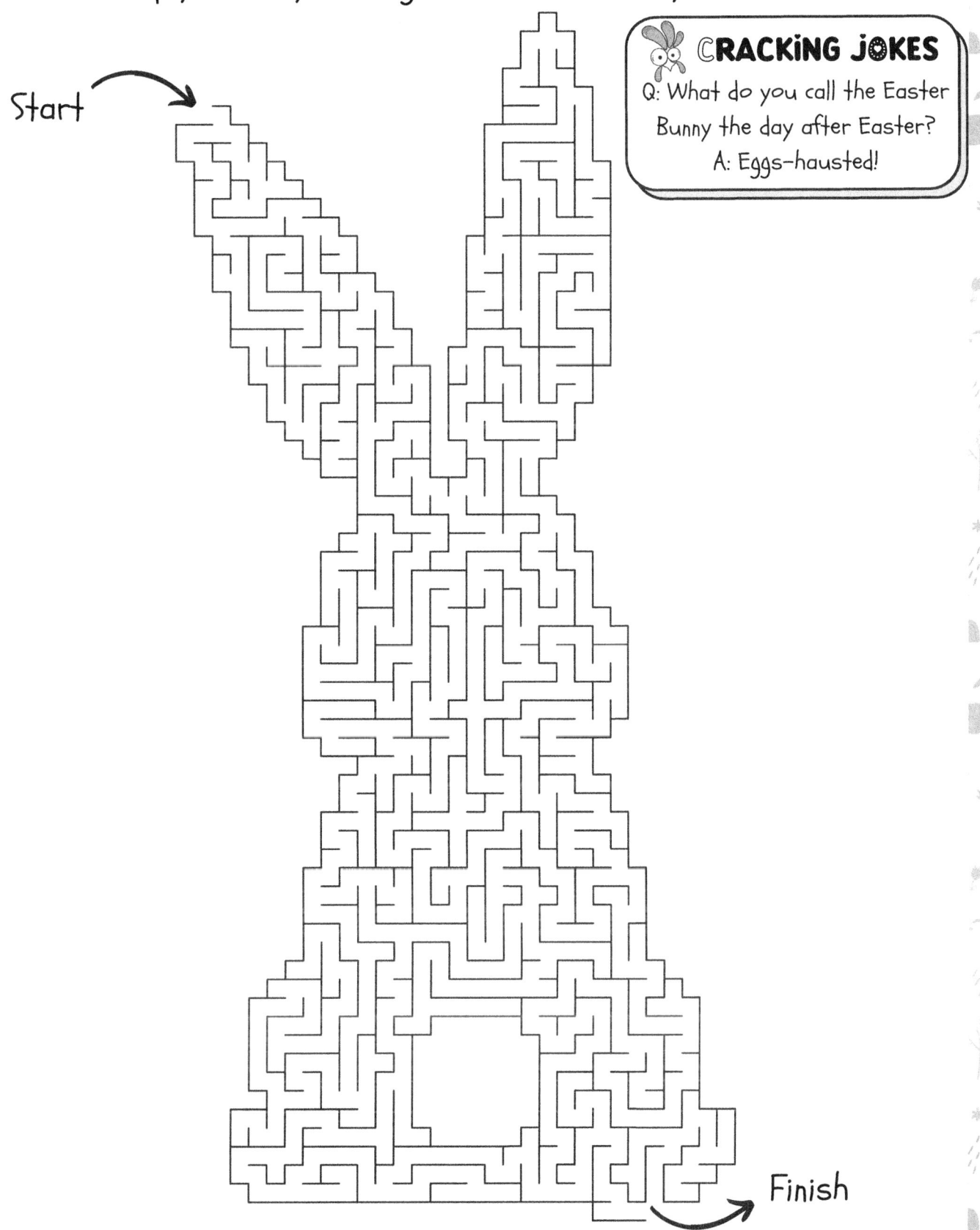

Start

Cracking Jokes
Q: What do you call the Easter Bunny the day after Easter?
A: Eggs-hausted!

Finish

47

Colour By Numbers

Match the numbers to the colours to complete this Easter picture.

Blue	Green	Brown	Yellow	Pink	Red	Orange
1	2	3	4	5	6	7

Broken Eggs

51

Oh no the eggs have all been knocked off the shelf! Let's get cracking and fix those broken eggs by drawing a line between the correct top and bottom pieces of each egg to put them back together again.

A.   B.    C.    D.

1.    2.    3.    4.

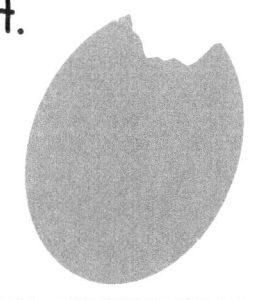

I have counted...

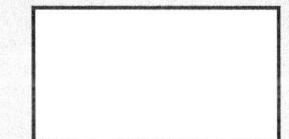

Easter eggs in and around this jar.

Spring Sums

Can you work out the value of each Spring flower and complete the calculations?

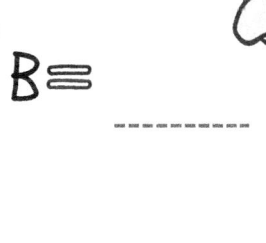

A. 
B. 
C.

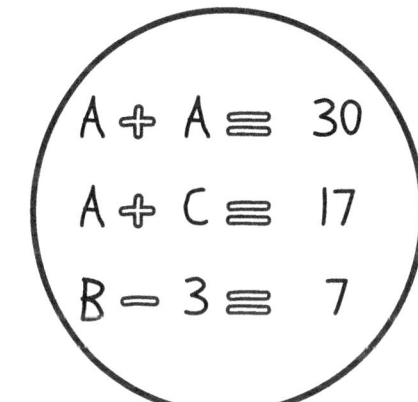

A + A = 30
A + C = 17
B − 3 = 7

A = _____
B = _____ 
C = _____

1.  🌼 + 🌻 + 🌹 = _____

2.  🌹 × 3 = _____

3.  🌹 + 🌼 − 🌻 = _____

4.  🌼 × 3 = _____

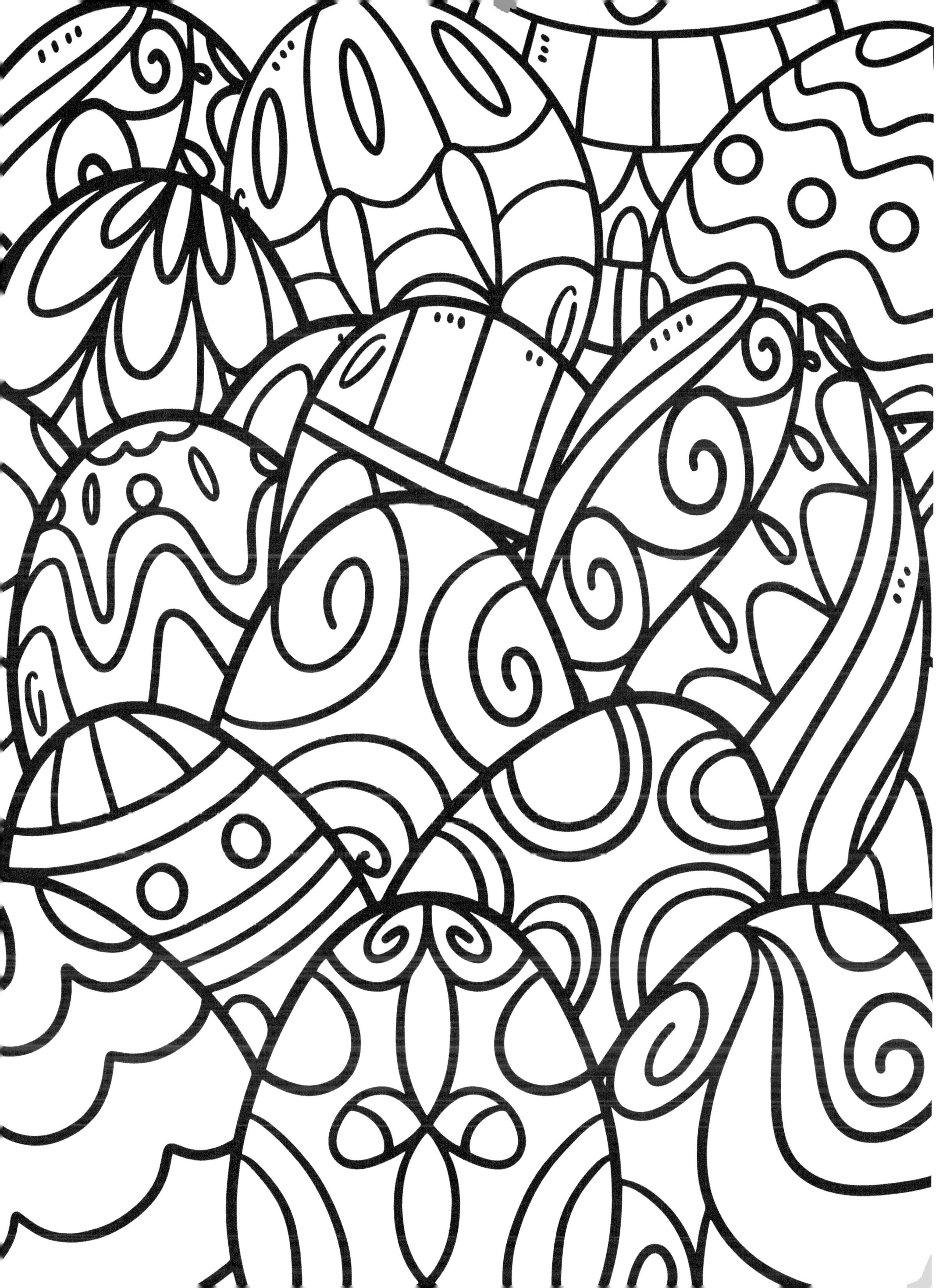

Escape Route

57

The farmer has caught the rabbit eating carrots! Can you be a-maze-ingly helpful and help the rabbit find an escape route through the underground maze?

Start

Finish

Draw a line matching the correct animal to their footprint.

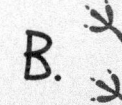

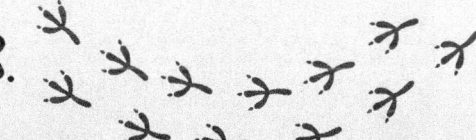

1.

2.

3.

A.

B.

C.

Race To find The Eggs

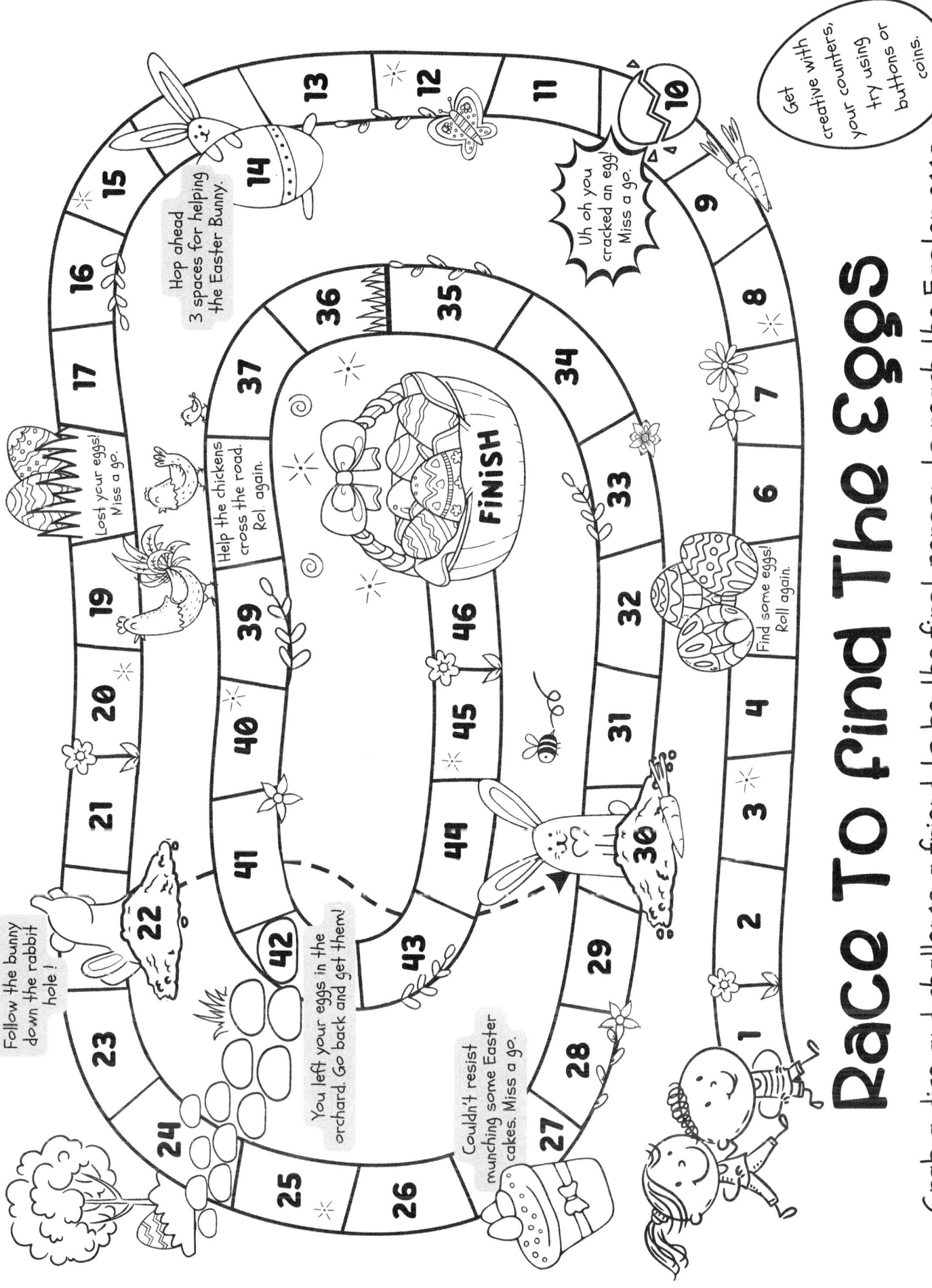

Grab a dice and challenge a friend to be the first person to reach the Easter eggs.

Get creative with your counters, try using buttons or coins.

Uh oh you cracked an egg! Miss a go.

Hop ahead 3 spaces for helping the Easter Bunny

Lost your eggs! Miss a go.

Follow the bunny down the rabbit hole!

You left your eggs in the orchard. Go back and get them!

Couldn't resist munching some Easter cakes. Miss a go.

Help the chickens cross the road. Roll again.

Find some eggs! Roll again.

Crossword Clues

It's time to put your egg-spertise to the test and see if you can unscramble this crossword puzzle using the clues found inside the Easter Eggs scattered around the page.

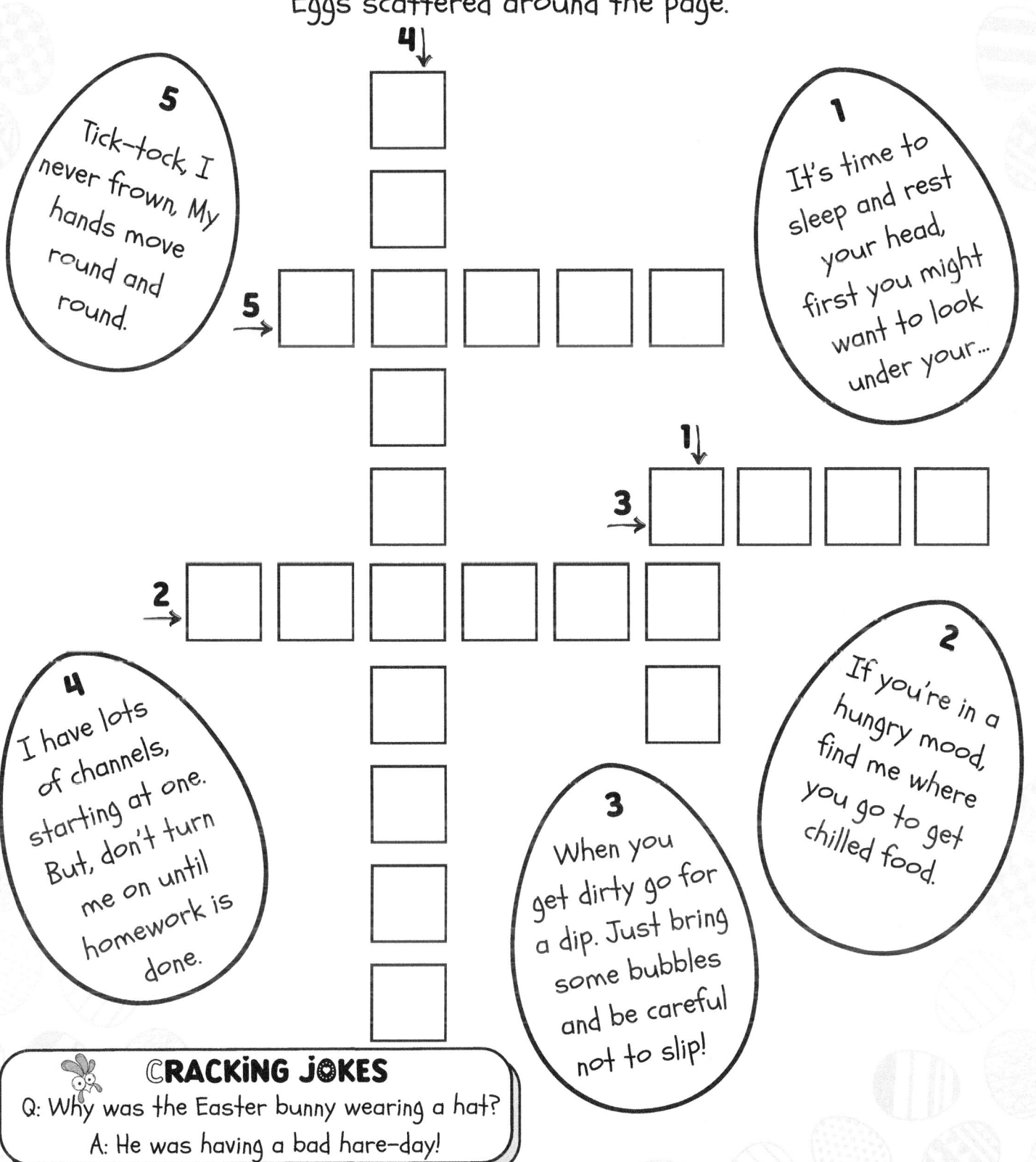

5 Tick-tock, I never frown, My hands move round and round.

1 It's time to sleep and rest your head, first you might want to look under your...

4 I have lots of channels, starting at one. But, don't turn me on until homework is done.

3 When you get dirty go for a dip. Just bring some bubbles and be careful not to slip!

2 If you're in a hungry mood, find me where you go to get chilled food.

CRACKING JOKES
Q: Why was the Easter bunny wearing a hat?
A: He was having a bad hare-day!

Crack The Code

Only one basket is full of chocolate eggs – the rest are hard-boiled! Crack the code and match it to the basket that has the sweet treats.

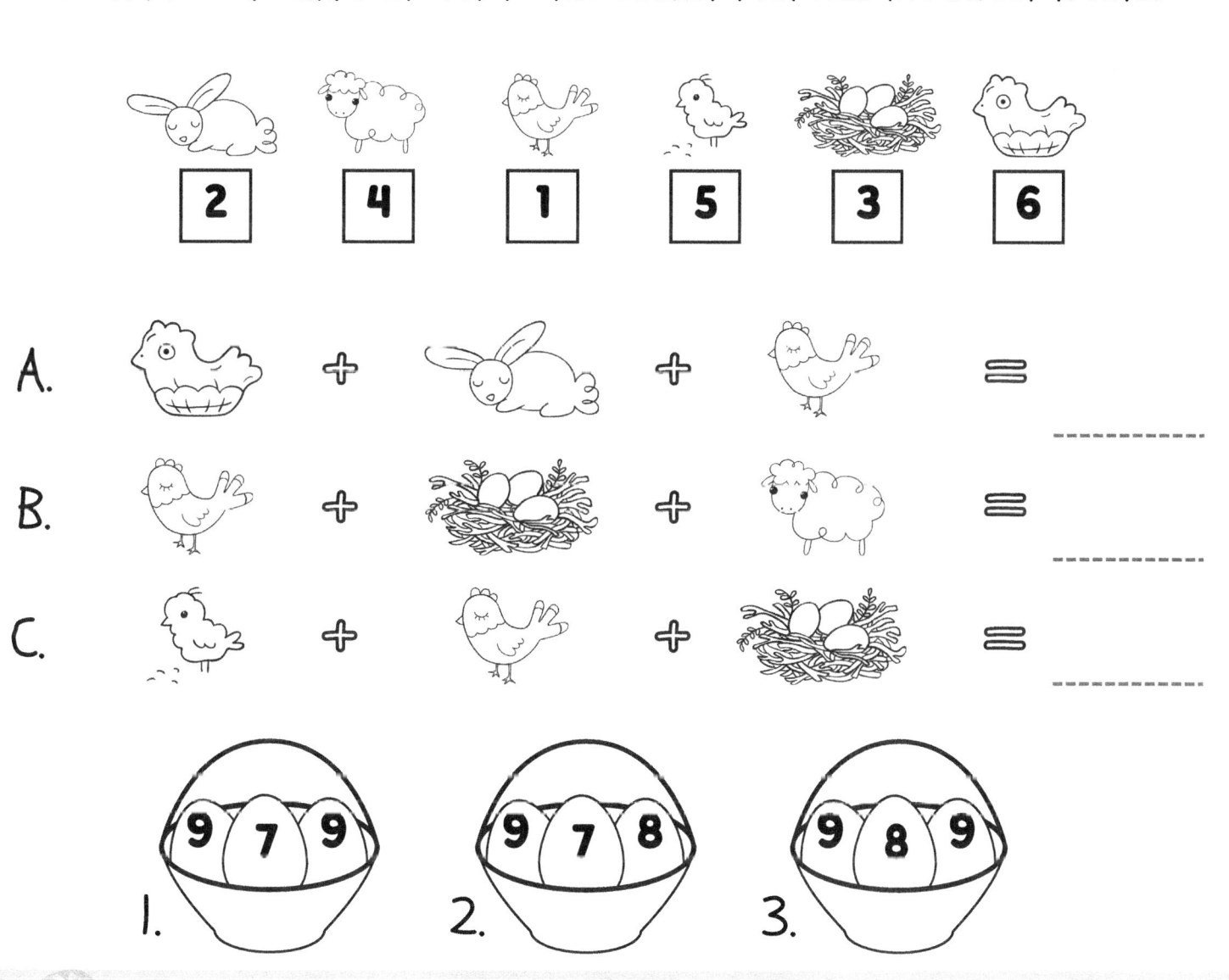

Bunny = 2, Sheep = 4, Chicken = 1, Chick = 5, Nest = 3, Hen in basket = 6

A. Hen + Bunny + Chicken = _____

B. Chicken + Nest + Sheep = _____

C. Chick + Chicken + Nest = _____

1. 9 7 9
2. 9 7 8
3. 9 8 9

One of these Easter bunnies is different. Circle the odd bunny out.

A.   B.   C.   D.

Somebunny's Escaping [65]

Hop to it and help our bunny friend find its burrow. Follow only the carrots through the garden, but remember, no hopping diagonally – even if you spot other tasty veggies along the way!

Start

Finish

CRACKING JOKES
Q: What jewellery does a bunny wear?
A: A 14-carrot gold necklace!

Doodle Chicks

Doodle over these blobs to create your own Easter chicks.

Just like me!

Or me!

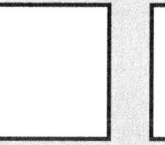

Can you find the answer to this riddle using the clues on each line?

What animal am I?

My first letter is in the word LIGHT and also in LOVE

My second letter is in the word BAD but <u>not</u> in BED

My third letter is in the word MARRY but <u>not</u> in CARRY

My fourth letter is in the word CRUMB and also in BAKE

I am a.... ☐ ☐ ☐ ☐

Primary Colours

69

The primary colours of red, yellow and blue are egg-stra special as they cannot be made from other colours. Colour in the two eggs below in only primary colours.

Did you know that when we mix two primary colours we get a secondary colour? These are orange, green and purple. Can you figure out which secondary colour you need to colour in these three eggs?

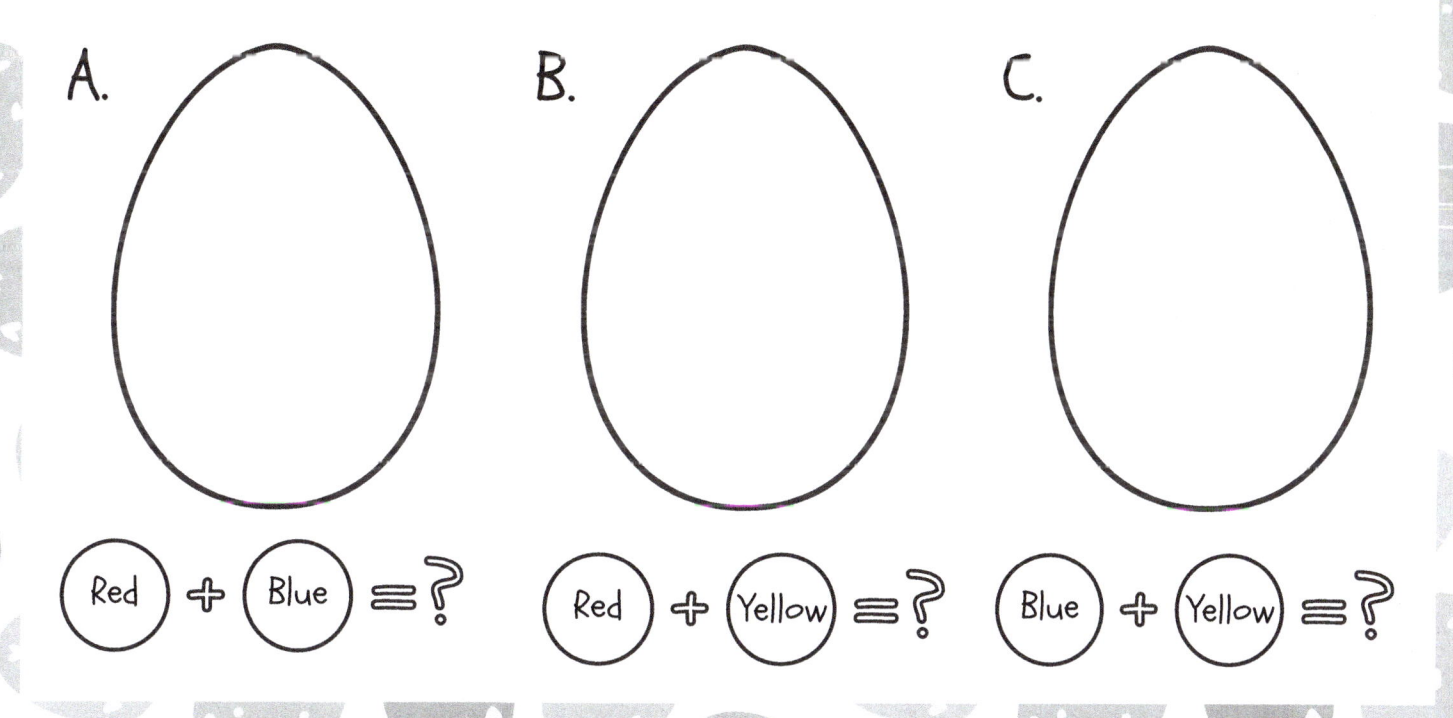

A.

B.

C.

Red + Blue = ?

Red + Yellow = ?

Blue + Yellow = ?

Spring Shadows

70

Draw a line matching these spring animals with their shadows. Can you spot the extra shadow?

1.
2.
3.
4.
5.

A.
B.
C.
D.
E.
F.

Complete the sequence by drawing what comes next.
Is it a cockerel, chicken or chick?

A   B   C   C   B   ?

Co-Ordinate Your Hunt 73

Check out the code below the blank box, then hunt for the egg matching those co-ordinates on the chart above. Write the letter inside the same box as the egg to unlock the answer to this clue.

7
6 a
5 t
4 f
3 b
2 h
1 l
   A B C D E F G

"I have four legs, but cannot walk
You sit at me when you use a fork..."

C,5	B,2	F,7	C,5	A,6	D,3	G,1	F,7

Easter Counting

Count how many of each item you can spot in the picture above.

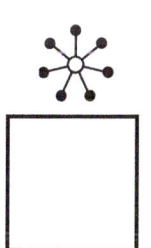

75

Chocolate Creations

Arrange these instructions into the correct order (steps 1-10) on the dashes below to unveil the process of making creamy chocolate! Get ready to unlock the sweet secrets behind everyone's favourite Easter treat!

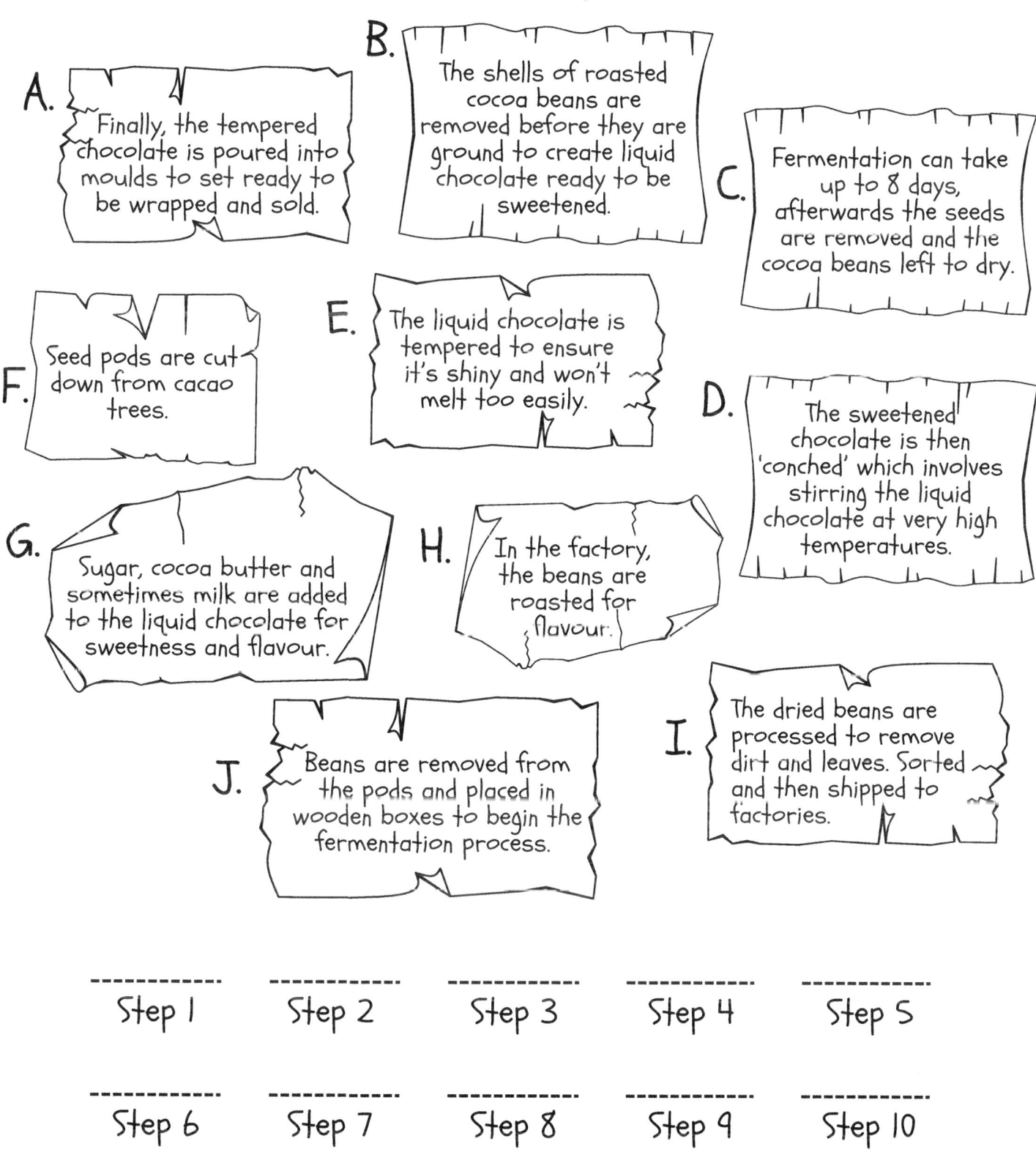

A. Finally, the tempered chocolate is poured into moulds to set ready to be wrapped and sold.

B. The shells of roasted cocoa beans are removed before they are ground to create liquid chocolate ready to be sweetened.

C. Fermentation can take up to 8 days, afterwards the seeds are removed and the cocoa beans left to dry.

D. The sweetened chocolate is then 'conched' which involves stirring the liquid chocolate at very high temperatures.

E. The liquid chocolate is tempered to ensure it's shiny and won't melt too easily.

F. Seed pods are cut down from cacao trees.

G. Sugar, cocoa butter and sometimes milk are added to the liquid chocolate for sweetness and flavour.

H. In the factory, the beans are roasted for flavour.

I. The dried beans are processed to remove dirt and leaves. Sorted and then shipped to factories.

J. Beans are removed from the pods and placed in wooden boxes to begin the fermentation process.

---------- ---------- ---------- ---------- ----------
Step 1   Step 2   Step 3   Step 4   Step 5

---------- ---------- ---------- ---------- ----------
Step 6   Step 7   Step 8   Step 9   Step 10

Easter Pop Up Scene

1) Colour in the two pictures.
2. Cut them out.
3) Fold down the dotted lines.
4) Glue the folded section of picture 1 to the matching letter on picture 2

Picture 1

Picture 2

ANSWERS

81

Page 4 – Easter Hunt

B – Behind the Barn

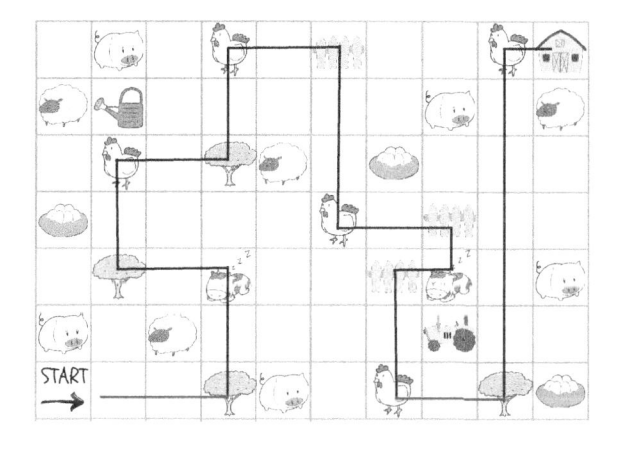

Page 9 – Egg-cellent Pairs

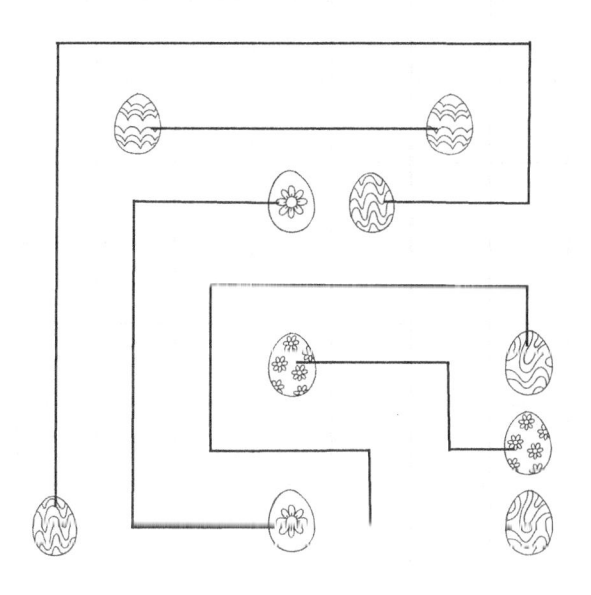

Page 11 – Secret Message

We hope you have a Happy Easter

Page 11 – Odd Tree Out

B

Page 13 – Egg-citing Maze

Page 15 – Spot the Difference

ANSWERS

Page 17 - Easter Riddle

ONLY ONE, AFTER THAT IT'S NOT EMPTY!

Page 21 - Match The Eggs

A-F, B-I, C-H, E-G

Odd Egg Out - D

Page 23 - Animals On The Loose

Page 23 - Scribbled Out Vowels

1 - Easter Egg Hunt

2 - Egg and Spoon Race

Page 27 - Odd Egg Out

C

Page 27 - Egg And Spoon Race

C

Page 33 - Easter Maths Riddle

They have TWENTY ONE Easter eggs in total

Page 43 - Easter Word Hunt

Page 45 - Scrambled Eggs

A - Daffodil

B - Basket

C - Chocolate

The hidden hiding place is the SHED

ANSWERS

Page 47 – Bunny Maze

Page 51 – Broken Eggs
A-3, B-4, C-1, D-2

Page 51 – Counting Eggs
There are 24 eggs

Page 53 – Spring Sums
A – 15, B – 10, C – 2

1) 5 + 10 + 2 = 27
2) 2 x 3 = 6
3) 2 + 15 – 10 = 7
4) 15 x 3 = 45

Page 57 – Escape Route

Page 57 – Connect Animals To The Right Footprint
1-B, 2-C, 3-A

Page 61 – Crossword Clue

Across:
2. FRIDGE
3. BATH
5. CLOCK

Down:
1. BED
4. TELEVISION

ANSWERS

Page 63 – Crack The Code

A) 6 + 2 + 1 = 9

B) 1 + 3 + 4 = 8

C) 5 + 1 + 3 = 9

The correct basket is 3

Page 63 – Odd Bunny Out

D

Page 65 – Somebunny's Escaping

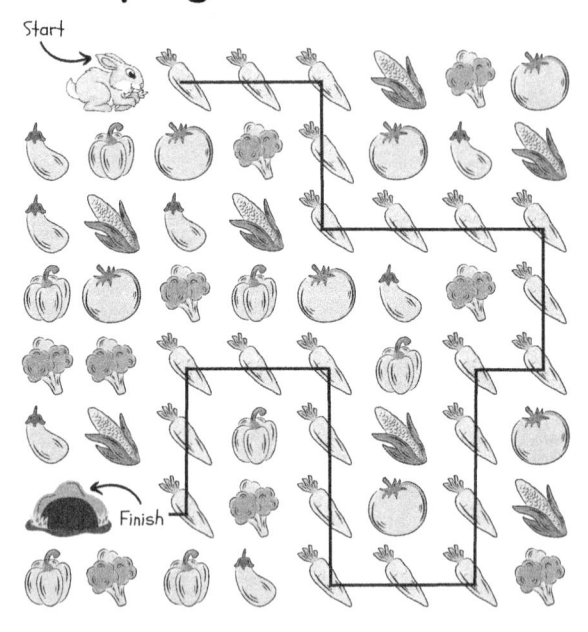

Page 67 – What Am I Riddle?

I am a LAMB

Page 69 – Primary Colours

A – Purple, B – Orange
C – Green

Page 70 – Spring Shadows

1–C, 2–F, 3–D, 4–B, 5–A

Page 70 – Odd Shadow Out

E

Page 70 – Chicken Pattern

A

Page 73 – Co-ordinate Your Hunt

THE TABLE

Page 75 – Easter Counting

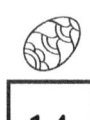

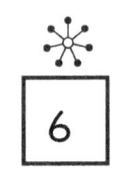

14, 4, 3, 3, 6

Page 77 – Chocolate Creations

Step 1 – F,   Step 6 – B
Step 2 – J,   Step 7 – G
Step 3 – C,   Step 8 – D
Step 4 – I,   Step 9 – E
Step 5 – H,   Step 10 – A

WE HOPE YOU HAD AN EGG-STRAORDINARY TIME!

Look out for more egg-citing activity books just for kids from Crumps Cottage Publishing.

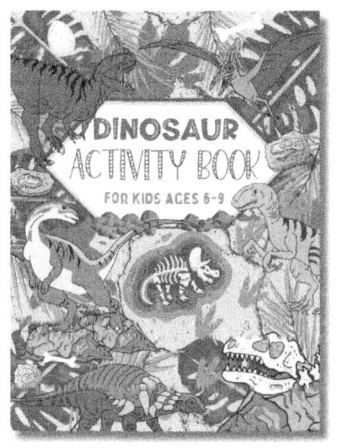

Printed in Great Britain
by Amazon